THE AUTHENTIC SELF

LEARN TO COACH YOURSELF TO ULTIMATE SUCCESS

By

Dr BRENDA HATTINGH

Book 2. Series
Authentic Living and Leading

Copyright © 2020 Dr. Brenda Hattingh.

All rights reserved.
No part of this book may be used, or reproduced and transmitted in any form or by any means, electronic or mechanical, including photocopying, recording, or by any information storage and retrieval system, without signed permission in writing from
the copyright owner and publisher.

Cover design by Zander Hattingh
Editing by Copywriting: David Barraclough
Quality Writing and Editing Services
Website: http://www.copy-writing.co.za.
Email: david.barraclough@copy-writing.co.za
Graphics by: Gerart Snyman
Email: info@gerart.co.za

ISBN: 9798551748243

Published by:
Currency Communications International. (Pty. Ltd.)
Johannesburg. South Africa.

Copies available on:
Amazon.com/books
E-books: website: http://www.brendahattingh.com
Audio books: Website: http://www.brendahattingh.com
For more information email: info@powerintelligence.net

CONTENTS

Sudden shutdown 6
- ☐ Coming to a standstill 6
- ☐ How many people can work on their own? 7
- ☐ What will the result of the global shutdown be? 7
- ☐ Returning to the new normal 8
- ☐ Preparing for 2020 8

The story behind the story 9
- ☐ Life defining events 9
- ☐ Becoming self-aware and self-responsible 10
- ☐ Busy schedule halted 10
- ☐ Being helpless and powerless 11
- ☐ The inner battle 11
- ☐ Discovering two sides of self 12
- ☐ Getting to know my self 13
- ☐ Our inner real-me-revolution 13
- ☐ Negotiating with God 14
- ☐ Reaching for higher guidance 14
- ☐ Given free will – the ability to choose 15

Conscious mindful decisions 16
Discovering the three S's of success 16
Overcoming the guilt trip 17
Taking back your power 17

- Detox, detangle, and redesigning my life 18
- Coaching others 19
- Many options 19
- Turning point 20
- Discovering the Human Genome Project 21
- Findings of the Human Genome Project 21
  - ☐ The God-gene hypothesis 22
  - ☐ Biological and spiritual hereditary 23
  - ☐ Original blueprint 23
  - ☐ Nothing is fixed – everything is in motion 24
  - Constant change and transformation 25
- Activating our DNA-blueprint 25
- DNA success-blueprint 26
- Keeping up – and staying ahead 26
- Who makes the decisions in your life? 27
- The outcome of your life 28
- You have the power to change 28
- Giving power to your decision-maker 29
- Coaching 30
- The importance of coaching 30
  - ☐ Why coaching? 31
  - ☐ Benefits of coaching 33
  - ☐ What a coach and life-strategist can do? 33
  - ☐ Finding what works best for you 34
  - ☐ Who is the life coach or strategist? 35
- What are the benefits of first having a personal coach? 36
- What are the benefits of having an organisational coach? 36
- Self-coaching: What is self-coaching? 38
  - ☐ Who coaches who? 38
  - ☐ Listen to your heart 39

- ☐ Getting to know the shadow ego-self..................................39
- ☐ Feeling ashamed...40
- ☐ Mastering your shadow ego-self..................................40
- ☐ Taking personal responsibility 41

The real-me, authentic self...42

Ego-centered versus Real-me centered living.....................43

Change is important..44

Summary 44

Gaining more clarity 46

Your To-do list 47

What is ultimate success?..48

What next?...50

Enroll for a 5-week self-coaching course........**Error! Bookmark not defined.**

Who is the author - Dr Brenda Hattingh? **Error! Bookmark not defined.**

OoooOooo

LEARN TO COACH YOUR SELF

Sudden shutdown

Without any warning, the world is in a total shutdown. The Coronavirus came out of no-where and within a couple of weeks, the planet was on red-alert.

Businesses, companies, organisations, public events, meetings, social gatherings, schools, colleges, borders, travel, holidays, and countless other gatherings were shut down within days.

- **Coming to a standstill**

Everything and everyone came to a standstill. Leaders, business owners, organisers, and even parents wonder: "What now? Will the country, the economy, business, especially small businesses, survive?"

We learn how dependent we are on our contact with others. Suddenly remote contact, the internet, social communications systems, and long-distance business management, become the optimum solution.

Important questions arise: How productive are people when they need to work on their own? What about our children? How self-sufficient are they?

- **How many people can function on their own?**

There are those people who are self-motivated, self-driven, and can remain productive while working on their own. This is however a very small percentage.

Not everyone is ready, willing, or able to work without supervision. Many still need support, motivation, and external help and guidance. Especially our children.

- **What will the outcome of the shutdown be?**

Global leaders, company owners, team managers, schoolteachers, and lectures, ask: Will our people, our teams, our students, be able to work on their own and remain productive during this shutdown? What about after this is over? Where will we stand? What will the result of the global shutdown be?

A more personal question is: Can you work on your own and still stay productive?

Some will say 'yes'. Others see this shutdown as an opportunity to stay at home and have an unplanned holiday. This is of deep concern to all responsible people.

The result will all depend on where you are coming from, where you want to go, what your vision is, and how you plan to get there. The time to learn to coach yourself to ultimate success – is here.

- **Returning to the new normal**

Once life returns to a new normal within a few weeks – countries, companies, organisations, institutes, and industries will need to assess the standing of their whole situation, especially their businesses. Important questions are: How much damage was done? How far behind are we? How productive are our people without supervision? What catching up needs to be done? What is the 'new normal'?"

A new challenge is to have people now trained in *Self-coaching*.

This is not a luxury – it has become a necessity.

- **Preparing for 2020**

Over the last few years, I have been preparing the books, training material, webinars, and coaching material, to help people to coach themselves to ultimate success.

What makes this more unique is that it includes activating your original DNA success-blueprint as part of self-coaching.

The plan was to launch it all in September 2020. Now that I look back … I realise there are no coincidences.

As you will find in the rest of this book, I stumbled onto my journey of self-coaching, by coincidence.

So, please join me on this journey of discovering how to coach yourself to ultimate success. I can guarantee you – it's an exciting ride…

The story behind the story.

The silent humming of the CAT scan machine initially was soothing and reassuring. However, a sudden overwhelming panic attack set off all the security monitors. Red lights and sirens all went off at the same time.

My inner sirens and red lights followed suit – everything was on red alert! Relief came when the doctor and nurse did what they needed to do and a silent calm settled in as the medication, did its work.

- **Life defining events**

Over the last weeks so much had happened. First, there was the pile-up on the highway. A speeding car smashed into our rear. Then a series of life-defining events followed that changed my life forever.

This took place a few years ago.

It was the death of an old life and the birth of a new beginning and a different kind of quality living. It also was the birth of this book ... and various others, including the course on self-coaching.

My hope is that this will help you to become aware of how important self-coaching is.

- ### Becoming self-aware and self-responsible

I realised that we are all personally responsible for our own health, wealth, and happiness and that quality of life is a personal choice. There are no victims!

Life is also fragile. Life is a gift. Life as you know it can change at any time and without any warning.

I became aware that I had to dig deep to find the power and courage to get up and get out of this dilemma.

Taking the proverbial 'bull by the horns' and coaching myself back to health and a new life, became my only choice and my new agenda.

I also became deeply aware that, in essence – I was on my own. I was alone in this. No-one else was going to do this for me.

- ### Busy schedule halted

My very large practice at the Eugene Marais Hospital in Pretoria, South Africa, and large private practice, coaching, and leadership-consulting business, were demanding responsibilities. I also lectured at the university and did research and development work.

As a wife, mother of four sons, a colleague, and a friend, I had to fill my place. At the same time, I was on various committees, involved in social development and literacy programs in rural areas, and did counselling work at the central prison. As an inspirational speaker, I also travelled a lot.

My diary was fully booked; I was overworked and very, very tired. There was no thought of slowing down before the end of the year.

Suddenly, it was all still.

- **Being helpless and powerless**

The pain in my right leg grew and grew, whilst excruciating headaches rendered me helpless. Over a few days, I had lost all feeling in my right leg. I became paralysed. I couldn't walk

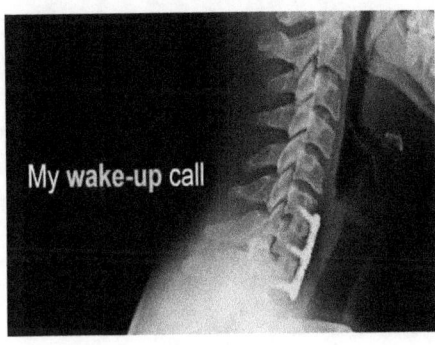

My wake-up call

The CAT-scan revealed three fractured neck vertebrae that needed an immediate neck-fusion. This put me out of circulation and out of work. It was a serious wake-up call. There was no other choice.

I was off the market and out of circulation, indefinitely..

- **The inner battle**

For more than a year I struggled with an inner battle. One part of me wanted to give up. The other part wanted to get up and get out of these circumstances.

Attached to a bed with tubes, screws, and steel support structures, I was powerless and helpless.

An inner real-me-revolution was raging in the silent chambers of my soul. Nobody knew. I was alone...

I was in an inner battle with myself.

- Discovering two sides of self

It is at this point that I realised we have two sides of self.

Some days I would feel despondent not being able to move. Just staring at the ceiling, made my brain work overtime.

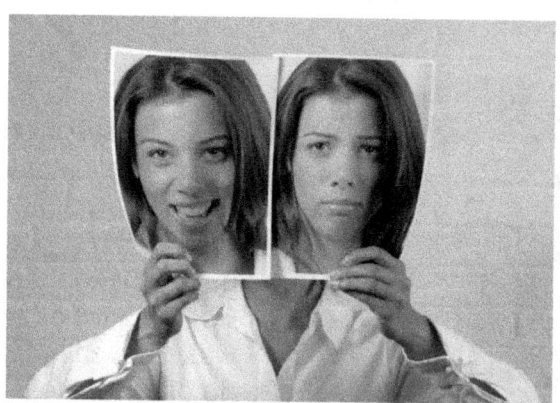

We all have two sides of self.

I soon realised that one side of self was prone to self-pity, depression, and anger, by constantly asking: "Why me?"

I realised that this was a negative and depressing part of the self who felt victimised and saw the cup half empty.

The biggest shock was when I realised – she is real!

- **Getting to know my self**

I decided to get to know this part of myself better. I saw her as my disconnected shadow ego-self. I named her – Elaine.

On the other hand – a different part of self would shine through from time to time. She saw the glass half full by bringing hope, motivation, and inspiration to heal, get up and stand up and once again fill my space on the marketplace.

I identified with this part of myself as my Real-me self. I felt I knew her and that this is who I was meant to be. I felt comfortable with her and I became aware that she was my real-me, authentic self. Her name is Brenda.

What a wonderful discovery.

- **Our inner real-me-revolution**

This inner battle between these two parts of self went on for nearly a year. This battle continues still to this day. I realised this is part of being human. Deal with it!

They were constantly communicating. It was something like a Netflix movie playing off in my head.

Sometimes I wondered who would win, and in the end, take over the control of my life. Some days, I wanted to give up and just die. Other days I couldn't wait to get up and start living again.

I became aware that an inner real-me-revolution was taking place. As a spectator – I had the final decision. Whichever side I chose to support, would grow and become my reality.

My future depended on this one choice:

Who would win my inner Real-me-revolution?

- **Negotiating with God**

Usually, we begin this journey of survival by grasping for straws outside of self. We expect someone to come and save us. We subconsciously become a 'victim' or a 'helpless patient' with the hope that others, even God, would feel sorry for us – and come to our rescue.

We even try to negotiate with God. We expect miracles.

Over time, when nothing happens, it starts to become clear – the Creator, Higher Power, Universal Source, God, or any other name you would like to use for a Deity – already gave us all the power and potential we need to lead a healthy quality life of success and happiness.

This is all encoded as our unique DNA success-blueprint and doesn't dissolve just because we are sick, in shock our incapacitated. It's always there.

- **Reaching for higher guidance**

This truth came to me when I, out of desperation, started reading various spiritual scripts. I was desperate and looking for higher guidance. I reached for my Bible…

Here I found the following:

> "The Kingdom of God is not one of Idle words
> The Kingdom of God is one of Power…."[1]
> further
> "First seek for the Kingdom that is within you
> …and the rest will be given unto you"[2]

This was the beginning of my journey within. It was also the beginning of my personal course in self-coaching. It was also the beginning of my recovery.

I started going within by learning about reclaiming my power, my health, my future while creating a new exciting life of happiness and fulfillment.

It was the birth of the book: *Power Intelligence – Mastering your miracle mind*.

My recovery had suddenly been fast-forwarded with leaps and bounds. I was excited and inspired to heal and get up and walk, as fast as possible.

I knew I still had daily battles to fight and choices to make.

- **Given free will – the ability to choose**

We were also gifted free-will. This is the ability to choose how we want to use our inner power, potential, and encoded DNA success-blueprint.

The choice is ours for the making – and the taking.

My decision was: I will do everything to win this inner battle, my real-me-revolution. I decided to let go of all negativity and heal. Together with my real-me self, we could create a whole new 5-Star life, that benefits everyone.

Mindfully and consciously I chose to get to know myself better. I chose to connect to and develop the real-me authentic self. I chose to bring the best self, my 5-star self to the table.

Just by silently making these inner choices, I felt my energy return. I was healing faster. Every day I became stronger and more motivated to get up and walk again. I was also inspired to bring this wonderful news to those who would listen.

My banner for my new life became:

'I'm daily winning my inner real-me-revolution by creating my 5-Star life and being of service to others.'

Conscious mindful decisions

I made a conscious mindful choice, to see this accident as an opportunity to let go of everything old and worn out. I started to reconsider the meaning of my life, my values, and my personal purpose.

For, although I was busy with making everyone happy and bettering their lives, I was overworked, unhappy, unfulfilled, and burnt out. In essence – I was lost in the mountains of work and service to others.

Discovering the three S's of success

I was forced to a standstill. Now it was time for a change. It was time for me. I also learnt the three steps in ultimate success: *Silence, Solitude, and Simplicity.*

A real, authentic leader like Nelson Mandela[3] also went through the three-S's before he became a global influencer. So, will everyone else who is on this journey of the unfolding of our power, purpose, and prosperity.

The Coronavirus has forced the world into silence, solitude, and simplicity. We will never be the same.

Overcoming the guilt trip

At first, I felt guilty about the new decision to use this opportunity to stop everything – and take care of me. I realised that this resistance came from my shadow ego-self.

Not only is this part of our self a sore loser – it fights back and struggles to maintain control. It won't let go of the delusional life it created, without a struggle.

This negative voice and influence needed to be silenced.

In the silence, it became evident that loving, caring, and nurturing yourself first, is the key to being of real, authentic service to others.

I first had to win my own inner real-me-revolution, quieten my mind, and get reconnected on all levels – before I could step out and be of service to others again.

Gone was all the doom and gloom. I was excited to get up and get back into life. A new future was beckoning…

Taking back your power

Making the best use of your time is one of the greatest gifts you can give to yourself. I now had the time to reconsider life, re-evaluate my comfort zone, revisit past achievements, accomplishments, and failures. I also took stock of all the people in my life.

As I identified who my real 'significant others' were, I also became aware of what they brought to my life and what I brought to their lives. This included friends, family, and colleagues.

I realised that people were in your life for a reason, season, and some for a lifetime. Not everyone is predestined to stay in your life forever.

The time had come to let go of outworn relationships.

I took back my power from old habits and long-lost relationships that had died many moons ago.

Detox, detangle, and redesigning my life

By detangling from destructive, toxic negative people, processes, and patterns, you can fast-forward your life.

Some people who stayed behind in my detangling thought I had lost my mind.

The truth is, this new vision of the next season of my future, became clearer. I decided to call it my 5-Star life.

Like many others who have gone through their 'detox, detangle and reclaiming your life' period, I went through my change, transformation and, a transition like a butterfly transforming and hatching

Getting detangled[4]   from a cocoon.

I learnt it was called the period of '*the dark night of the soul.*'

Coaching others

Learning to detox your inner life of erroneous thoughts, defeating emotional patterns, and negative destructive habits are not that easy. Detangling from an old outworn and restrictive lifestyle was just as difficult.

It was clear how many others also silently struggled with these steps of getting to know yourself, to detox, detangle and redesign their lives, that I once again decided to go back to my life-coaching practice.

I could now show my new clients how to re-invent themselves and create a whole new quality life, step for step because I had walked the path myself.

I was happy for the many months cloistered to a bed, as it was an opportunity to learn first-hand what to do and how to do it.

Many options

There were many other roads I could have taken. I have colleagues and friends who could have helped me – but I didn't ask them. The reason is, I already knew what they would say - because that would be what I would say.

So, I decided to speak to myself as if I was a client who had just survived a serious accident and needed my help, support, coaching, mentoring, love, compassion, and care.

I would become more than a coach to myself – I would also be a nurse, a confidant, an understanding caretaker, and a loving friend. It all came freely …

The decision was to coach myself, not only back to health, but also back into life. But… not just any old life of survival. No, a 5-Star life with all the trimmings, bells, and whistles and happiness was where I wanted to go.

I would also help others to do the same …

Writing it all down

Fortunately, I wrote down every step I personally took, with the hope I could share it with others who also were committed to coaching themselves back to a quality 5-Star life.

This is what this series of books, workshops, and training courses are all about.[5] I am happy and very proud to say – these steps work. I know: 'I've been there, done that, got the tee-shirt'. I also reached a further turning point…

Turning point

Sometimes, in the deepest and darkest despair - comes a turning point. My turning point came early in the morning when I couldn't sleep. Reading through the latest scientific and medical developments, I stumbled upon the results of the Human Genome Project.

Having a B.Sc. degree in natural and medical sciences, with genetics, neuroscience, and neuropsychology, I found this information, fascinating.

It took me back to long hours in the lab, behind the microscope while discovering a whole new world through the lens of the electron-microscope.

Discovering the results of The Human Genome Project[6] was my turning point. I wouldn't have had time for this reading unless I was pinned to the bed. I was grateful for the opportunity.

Discovering the Human Genome Project

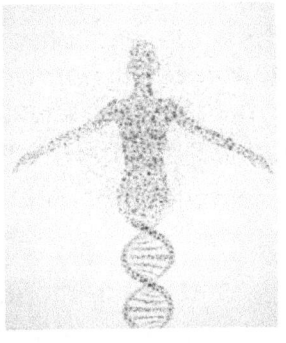

The results of the global research project into identifying the Human Genome became more available from 2000.

The purpose of the Human Genome Project was to unravel the coiled human DNA, straighten it out, identify disconnected parts, and the influence this has on our power, potential, and health. The aim was further to identify what a fully functional human genome would look like if all the parts were connected and fully functional.

Findings of the Human Genome Project

Astonishing findings were made through the Human Genome Project research. Some of the findings related to healing illnesses, preventing deterioration and preventing people from becoming sick. Still today, new findings are emerging and evolving from this project.

However, the results went much further than just physical health and immunity, it also included emotional, mental, and spiritual health and the influence of consciousness on our DNA.

- **The God-gene hypothesis**

It has been found that the ability to live in faith is partially heritable. This led to the 'God gene hypothesis'[7] that proposes that human beings inherit a set of genes that predisposes them to believe in a higher power.

This idea was postulated by geneticist Dean Hamers, the director of the Gene Structure and Regulation Unit at the U.S. National Cancer Institute.

He wrote a book on the subject titled: *The God gene: how faith is hardwired into our genes.* The God gene hypothesis is based on a combination of behavioural genetic, neurobiological, and psychological studies.[8]

The major arguments of the theory are:

- Spirituality can be quantified by psychometric measurements.
- The underlying tendency to spirituality is partially heritable.
- Part of this heritability can be attributed to the gene VMAT2.
- This gene acts by altering *monoamine* levels.
- Spirituality arises in a population because spiritual individuals are favoured by natural selection.

However, a few scientists and researchers are highly critical of this theory and some disputes followed.

The fortunate part is that these disputes placed the focus on the fact that there is an interconnectedness between genetics and spirituality and spiritual heredity. Spiritual awareness and raising consciousness have healing and genetic implications. The consequences of these findings have far-reaching effects for the everyday person in the street.

- **Biological and spiritual hereditary**

Biological heredity and biological families are now making way for spiritual heredity and a new spiritual family.

Life-long struggles with not fitting in with your biological family now make way for re-identification with a spiritual family that goes far beyond traditional teachings, religious dogma, biological genes, or that 'blood is thicker than water'. Another result is one of 'adoption'.

'Adoption' refers to the ability to choose for oneself. We have free-will to choose in which 'family' we want to be and with whom we want to be associated with. New choices include choosing to which spiritual family you want to belong to.[9] Choices are made through the heart.

Traditional religion is now being tested for universal spirituality.

- **Original blueprint**

Surprisingly, our original DNA-blueprint of health, wealth, happiness, and success, now becomes visible through the Human Genome Project.

What also becomes visible is that blockages and genetic disconnections are preventing us from fully utilizing our original power, full potential, and DNA success-print. This was not all…

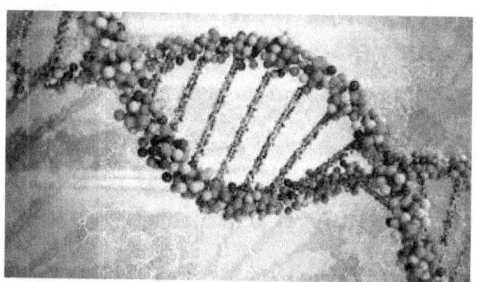

Our original DNA success-blueprint

- **Nothing is fixed – everything is in motion**

What was also found is that we have clock genes that can switch 'on' or 'off' at certain stages in our lives. We also have 'gene-migration' and even 'gene-jumping'.

From experience, we know that our DNA gets fragmented by experiencing traumatic experiences. DNA can also be healed and reconnected when you do the necessary inner work and consciously focus on taking back your power and healing your DNA.

DNA can also be healed by experiencing love and compassion.

We learn that nothing is fixed and even our DNA is constantly changing. Everything is switching on and off, duplicating, growing, dying off, being triggered, and activated. This is life in action!

Constant change and transformation

We are constantly going through a transformation.

Every second, growth, disintegration, death, and rejuvenation are taking place. Only our DNA success-blueprint is fixed. This is our original unique gift.

Just think, we have new skin-cells forming every day. Denser substances like bone take up to seven years to rejuvenate. This means that every seven years we could have a whole new body – if we kept to our original DNA-blueprint.

Unfortunately, we became disconnected, we grow old, our DNA unravels, and we age. Now it is time for not only a transformation, but also transcendence.

Activating our DNA-blueprint

At the same time, we learn that we can consciously influence these processes and activate some of the dormant parts of our DNA blueprint – if we know-how.

With the right emotional, mental, and spiritual toolkit, we can take part in our own transformation, healing, and welfare. We can even influence the rate of our aging.

When we overcome and take back our power from our shadow ego-self, we elevate our thinking and understanding. We can upgrade who we are – just like we upgrade our cellular phones.

We can learn to co-create a quality 5-Star life with all the gifts the Universe has gifted us.

I realised I needed to get up and bring this wonderful news to every-one who is open to listen – and hear. I had a new, exciting purpose.

In the next E-books and accompanying webinars and courses, we will take it step-for-step. You will learn how to get reconnected, activate your DNA blueprint, power, and potential and even turn difficult circumstances around.

DNA success-blueprint

What is most important is that we have an initial gift of a unique DNA success-blueprint encoded as part of my real-me authentic self. It is our original given blueprint.

As human beings, we are all flawed. This means everyone is disconnected at some or other level. This part of the self is just waiting to be activated.

Now – is the beginning of a new decade. The future is already here. It's the time of an approaching tsunami of rapid change and transformation. Our challenge is to be able to think on our feet.

The question is: Are you ready?

Keeping up – and staying ahead

The only way we can keep up is by learning to coach ourselves.

Some will be able to ride this wonderful wave of new energy, change, transformation, progress, and prosperity.

Unfortunately, some will stay behind.

The questions are: Who will be able to ride this wave? Who will be overcome by change? Who will stay behind?

Riding the waves of change by coaching yourself

The direction you go will be determined by which part of yourself makes the final decisions in your life.

Who makes the decisions in your life?

To understand which part of self is controlling your life – your first need to identify your different parts of self.

There are fundamentally two main parts. On the one hand, you have a connected, real-me authentic self. On the other hand, you find the disconnected, shadow ego-self.

Each part of the self is formed in different ways, with different points of view, different goals, values, and lifestyles. One side is negative and depressive – the other side is positive and uplifting.

They are constantly in communication. The truth is, they are essentially in a struggle or rather, in a battle, with each other.

Whoever wins the battle gets the last say and can make the decisions in your life. Every decision takes you in a specific direction. This determines the outcome of your life.

The outcome of your life

The outcome, quality, and success of your life is the result of hundreds, even thousands, of smaller decisions, that have collectively taken you to where you are now. It will continue unless you change the decision-making process.

You might erroneously think that external circumstances are responsible for the quality of your life. The truth is – irrespective of circumstances – you still make the decisions about the quality of your life.

If you want to change the quality of your life, you need to change your inner talk and decision-making processes. You can even change your programming on a DNA-level.

You have the power to change

You have the power to do make these new decisions.

This is actually very easy, as you are just returning to your original DNA-blueprint state of health, wealth, happiness, and success.

However – the shadow ego-self is a hard taskmaster that makes it difficult to let go of the old and create a new life. The Shadow-dweller always wants to win the battle – irrespective of how delusional it is. Its mere existence depends on it. It will keep on resisting your new efforts. It's this inner battle you first need to win.

Giving power to your decision-maker

As the 'spectator' of your life, you need to decide to whom you will give the power to make the final decisions.

You only have one of two choices:

On the one hand - you can decide to go with your shadow ego-self that is disconnected and living in the dark or different shades of grey. This will guarantee an easier path, but it leads to self-destruction.

Your choice is: *To do what is easy – or to do what is right.*

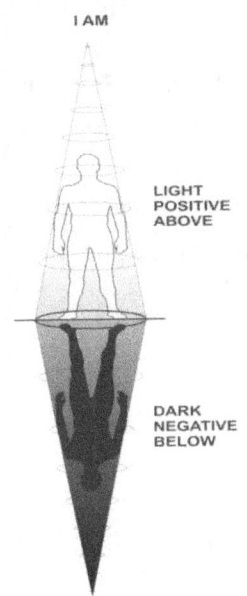

On the other hand, you can put all your efforts into getting reconnected to your authentic real-me self. By now you know it also holds your DNA success-blueprint. Doing all the self- or inner work holds many benefits.

Success is guaranteed.

The decision you will make – is your personal choice. Just remember – wherever you are coming from – will determine where you are going.

The quality of your life depends on this one important decision. You have freedom of choice.

Choose well…

The two sides of self

Finding answers to important questions

Now that you know how important this one decision is - the following questions arise:

1. How do I identify my real-me authentic self?
2. How do I identify my shadow ego-self?
3. How do I know who initially coaches who?
4. How can I change my patterns if I realise my shadow ego-self is winning the real-me-revolution?
5. What must I know about quality 5-Star living?
6. How do I create a quality 5-Star life for me and my loved ones?
7. How can I help others to discover their DNA Success-blueprint and 5-Star living so that it can benefit all?
8. How do I become a 5-Star leader – an authentic leader?

Answering all these questions is what this E-book, webinar and course, and all the other E-books, webinars, and courses to follow, will answer step for step.

Make sure you are enrolled in one of the courses. Make sure you are on our mailing list. So, the questions are: What is coaching and especially self-coaching.?

Coaching

The importance of coaching

As time speeds up – we need to learn to think on our feet while making quality, 5-Star decisions. Coaching is the ideal way to speed up this process. If you have the right coach – you can even activate your success-blueprint – right down to a DNA-level.

Coaching is one of the fastest-growing needs and therefore one of the fastest-growing professions in the world. It is estimated that 90% of Fortune 500 companies in the USA make use of coaches and 70 % of top companies in the UK provide coaching support to their staff.

Personal development is not only an organizational issue but fore and foremost a personal responsibility.

Life is becoming more and more complex and we need a deeper understanding, openness, and support. Coaching is therefore here to stay.

- **Why coaching?**

Research suggests that only a small percentage of people, truly feel motivated, committed, and positive about their success, well-being, prosperity, and the future.

The incidence of 'burn-out', depression, stress, and stress-related illnesses, are on the increase. This not only negatively influences productivity in teams, organisations, and companies, but personal health, happiness, and fulfillment are inhibited as well.

On the other hand, there are those persons who have come a long way.

They are successful, energetic, competent, and leaders in their fields. They have discovered the complexity of life and understand the personal need for someone to listen, understand, challenge, and soundboard.

They too do however need a professional, trustworthy, honest, and competent listener, to help them.

Tapping into the benefits of coaching[1]

By challenging old thinking, new vistas can open while reaching new heights, discovering new avenues, and developing new potential.

If you are one of these persons who would love some new input. The answer is – stop! You don't always need to go it alone.

Start by getting a trustworthy, qualified, competent coach and life-strategist to help you move to a new level.

You might even find someone who is capable and informed enough to help you coach yourself and access your DNA blueprint. Very few coaches and mentors have this know-how.

Once you are competent enough, you can coach yourself on your own. Know that at least, there is backup if you need a soundboard.

- **Benefits of coaching**

Most people do not know how to change their lives for the better, on their own. A lack of knowledge, skills, and tools cause people to shut down and/or give up. They're left stagnating in a dead-end – be it in a life-situation, health-issue, relationship, job, or any other situation.

The same applies to teams, companies, organisations, and even countries.

The truth is you don't have to suffer alone.

- **Stop doing more of the same**

Some keep on doing more of the same and stagnate in the process. Then there are the executives, managers, leaders, and people from all walks of life who are searching for a shorter, better and more elegant way to get where they want to be.

All these persons can benefit from the assistance of a life coach and/or business-strategist, to help and assist them in discovering personal potential, vision, and purpose, devise a strategy, develop a practical process, turn the new vision and plan into action, and to reclaim health, wealth, success, and happiness.

The same applies to teams, companies, organisations, and businesses.

- **What a coach and life-strategist can do?**

A life coach can be compared to a co-pilot. that supports, helps, challenges, directs, and assists the pilot in safely getting to the planned destination.

Your life too has a specific purpose and destination. So do teams, companies, organisations, and businesses, have an aim, focus, and purpose.

This is also constantly changing and needs to be revisited and constantly renewed to keep up with the times.

With our complex society, we find it more and more difficult to determine exactly what the purpose of a person, team, organization, or even a country, is.

People need to adapt to change by developing a new set of rules, without losing the self in the process. It is, therefore, necessary to keep track of who you are, where you are going, and why. Remember, you are also constantly changing, growing, and developing.

- **Finding what works best for you**

The professional Life Coach and Strategist can help you to learn what works best for you, identify what doesn't work, and avoid many pitfalls. A coach can help you with short-cuts and how to discover your personal vision, purpose, and passion.

Together you can identify an appropriate plan of action by tapping into inner resources, identify and change disempowering beliefs, turn stumbling blocks into steppingstones, embrace and effectively deal with challenges, change, transition, conflict, and setbacks.

They can help you to embrace the opportunities, improve work-performance, relationships, self-esteem, energy, focus, take calculated risks, resolve relationship and career crisis, and develop a balanced lifestyle of vision, success, happiness, and personal development

In the process, you will become connected, centered, balanced, and gain inner peace, and flexibility.

- **Who is the life coach or strategist?**

The coach is someone who has already walked a path and learnt from 'earth school'".

They are knowledgeable, informed, mature, willing, and able to be your co-pilot for a while.

Make sure you get the best coach for your needs and that you are a 'fit'.

Getting the benefits of your personal life coach[10]

Personally, they are good listeners, honest, courageous, and effective in providing feedback. They are visionary and analytic and can get to the core of issues.

They can help you plan, develop, and support practical solutions to problems that are followed up and brought to closure. Professionally they can be qualified in different areas of Human Sciences and make use of other professions and expertise, as necessary.

In the beginning, you might need a life-coach to show you the ropes. Just like a pilot, you can fully take over the controls when you are competent and feel comfortable enough.

What are the benefits of first having a personal coach?

At the beginning of this journey, you might need some help to get going with the short cuts to self-coaching.

By visiting a professional Life Coach, you create an opportunity to step back and take a new look at yourself and your life.

You become the spectator, scriptwriter, director, and producer of your own 'movie'. Visiting a coach helps you redefine your personal, career, relationship, life purpose, and goals.

If the person is qualified enough, they can help you redefine your next season of life and how to make it happen by tapping into your DNA Success-blueprint

You first need to know who you are, why things are happening in your life, and what you want, before, deciding where you want to go.

It's sometimes difficult to find this all out on your own.

Coaching sensitises people to think and act strategically in creating the lifestyle they desire.

What are the benefits of having an organisational coach?

Businesses, teams, companies, and organizations are living entities made up of living breathing people in the form of unified groups and teams – hopefully, functioning as a successful whole.

If not, the team and organisation will head for disaster.

Team and organisational coaching are especially necessary in major times of change.

Organisational coaching helps build the individuals into a fully functioning, self-organizing, business network.

Today it is a necessity for leaders to ensure that their, team, company, or organisation to upgrade their DNA Success-profile. Very few academics, facilitators, and/or trainers, know how to do this. We also need leaders to upgrade their DNA while developing a New Leadership DNA.[11]

Personal and team coaching motivates people to come together. Coaching is especially important at the most senior level in organizations.

It's lonely at the top and the board or senior management team also needs motivation and support. Very few people and business coaches are experienced enough to fulfill this role.

An objective outside coach can provide a climate of safety, security, and trust to the individual and can play a unique role as an interpreter while different groups and individuals grapple with complex challenges and questions.

Life has become too complex to make it alone…. and we don't have to. A competent coach can assist in the process until you are competent enough to coach yourself.

Self-coaching: What is self-coaching?

When we take our information about coaching above, into consideration – we realise that the more conscious, self-aware, mindful, and competent we become – we can replace the role of the external life-coach with our own inner life-coach, guide, and mentor.

We can learn to coach ourselves. We can learn to think on our feet.

A few things need to happen to get to this level: You first need to:

- Become self-aware. Get to know who you truly are
- Get connected and become your own best friend
- Become the silent, objective observer of your life
- Accept responsibility for writing the script for your new season.
- Become the director and producer of your own 'movie'
- Learn new skills and tools to be your own best coach ever. In the beginning, get help if necessary
- Remember where you come from …

- **Who coaches who?**

Now we can begin to answer this question.

Whoever you give decision-making power to, will coach you on the path of life. This is a challenge to stay diligent.

Our challenge is to be conscious of where we are coming from. We need to be certain of what our point of departure and approach to the self and life is.

As said, there are only one of two possibilities:

We either come from our disconnected, shadow ego-self – or our connected, enlightened, real-me, authentic self.

We must get to know both parts of self before we can choose who is in charge. This is not always that easy. We could get confused about who it is whispering in our ear, what we need to do.

We must develop inner discernment.

- **Listen to your heart**

An easy rule of thumb is: The shadow ego-self comes from your head. The real-me authentic self comes from your heart. Listen to your heart. Listen to and with your heart.

Getting to know yourself could and does sometimes, take a whole lifetime.

So, let's start by getting to know a bit about the two sides of self.

- **Getting to know the shadow ego-self**

Each of us has parts of the self that have been disconnected, splintered, or 'broken off'. We have not yet discovered, identified with, connected to, healed, grown, developed, or evolved in these fragmented areas.

This means parts of us are still on the dark or shadow side and most people live from a fragmented or disconnected self. These are your blind-spots

These parts are still 'stuck' somewhere in the past and are constantly seeking attention and invading our lives.

These parts want to be heard, acknowledged, and resolved. This reflects in the many fragmented and unhappy lives, relationships, careers, and businesses around us.

Most people are ignorant about or neglect to do the inner work while reincorporating the fragments and learning from their shadow self.

- **Feeling ashamed**

This happens mostly because we are – or unaware or ashamed of these parts that are not 'up to standard'. We rather choose to deny and ignore their existence. This drains much of our personal power and prevents us from moving forward.

A deep life-lesson is: *'Denial – is not the river in Egypt.'*

- **Mastering your shadow ego-self**

However, connecting to and taking conscious control of the shadow self is a very valuable step in reclaiming your power while growing in self-master and maturity.

If not, the shadow self continues to dominate our personal dynamics while influencing the path of our lives negatively and destructively. You will be lazy, unmotivated, without vision or purpose, lack direction, mostly frustrated, angry, or even burnt-out and depressed.

Remember – we all have a shadow ego-self. It's part of being human. It's nothing to be ashamed of – unless you like your dark side and let it loose to harm others.

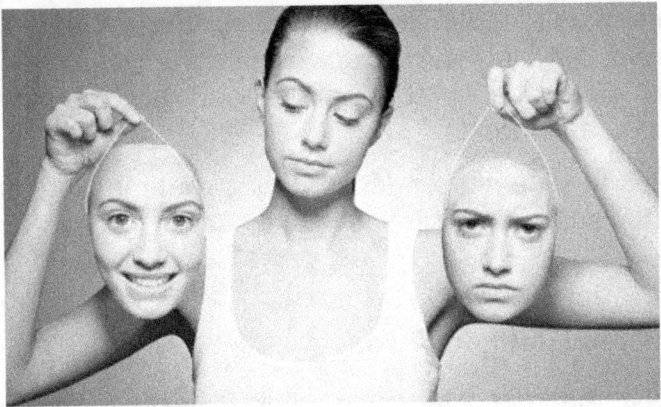

Master your shadow ego-self

The only difference between shadow dwellers and real-me livers is the fact that some people don't know or don't care that they are on a downward spiral.

Others are now waking up, taking note, and becoming conscious that they have a personal responsibility to master the dark side and grow the real-me self while creating a better life.

Not only the Coronavirus is shaking things up.

- **Taking personal responsibility**

At some time or another – everyone must stop and take personal control and responsibility for the quality of their lives.

This begins when we can face our shadow side and ego-self and consciously open-up, expose and heal our negative aspects. We first need to overcome our fears.

In the process, we become reconnected to the healed, whole, holy, original, real-me, authentic self.

At the same time, our New Success DNA[12] reconnects as well. We not only take back our power, but we also reclaim our authentic spark of life, and get our authentic self, back as a bonus.

So, let's take a closer look at our real-me, higher, or authentic self.

The real-me, authentic self

We have heard so much about the original real-me or 'authentic self' that we are compelled to ask the following important questions:

- What is the 'authentic self'?
- Where is it?
- What does it look like?
- Why did we lose this part of self?
- How do we find it and reconnect again?
- How do I create a new season in my life by coming from my real-me self?

Over the next few months, we will be releasing E-books that explain the answers to these questions. We also have courses accompanying each E-book in the Self-coaching series, to help you grow with each step.

Stay connected by making sure you are on our mailing list HERE [13]

The more you know and the more skills and tools you develop – the easier it becomes to coach yourself.

What we can identify so far is the kind of life we will lead by following one of our two choices

The Shadow ego-self leads to self-destruction while the Real-me soul-self leads to self-mastery and victory.

Remember- one side comes from your heart. The other side comes from delusional thoughts in your head.

Ego-centered versus Real-me centered living

The summary below indicates one of the two paths you could follow. Seven steps correspond to the seven steps of our developmental milestones.

This is outlined in the book New Success DNA.[14]

In other books, we will take it step-for-step in discovering the real-me self while overcoming the delusion of the shadow ego-self.

REAL-ME CENTRED Soul-self	EGO-CENTRED Shadow-self
Self-aware	Self-conscious
Self-worth	Self-centered
Self-esteem	Self-importance
Self-care	Self-serving
Self-confidence	Self-delusion
Self-respect	Self-indulgence
Self-mastery	Self-destructive

Soul-centred versus ego-centered living

Here you will find all the necessary tools and skills to change your life to the resonance of love, light, power, wisdom, and abundance.

For now – study this summary above. Ask yourself: Who makes the decisions in your life? The answer will show you where you can expect to finish up in the end.

Change is important.

Understand who is winning your inner Real-me-revolution. Be aware and know who is coaching who. Change as necessary to secure a bright future …

However, this not only means change and transformation, it also includes transcendence – moving to a whole new level.

Summary

Ask yourself: Where are you, your family, friends, staff, boss, leaders, children, teachers, or 'significant others', coming from?

Let's put the differences between the real-me and shadow ego-self side by side. This will make it easier for you to tick off what you have already developed and what still needs to be done.

It also makes it easier to see where your business colleagues, boss, team, company, and/or organisation are coming from.

Whatever adds up to be the most prominent in your life – is bound to become your reality…and your future.

Decide who you are: I am…

REAL-ME AUTHENTIC SELF	SHADOW EGO-SELF
Connected	Half- or Disconnected
Centered	Off or unbalance
Grounded	Ungrounded/ floating
Real and authentic	Delusional /plastic
Has vision /Focussed	No vision/ unfocussed
Happy and fulfilled	Unhappy /unfulfilled

Has purpose	Hasn't identified purpose
Self-motivated	Seeks external motivation
Inspired/ own energy	Uninspired/ drain others
Has work ethic	No or low work ethic
Can work alone	Must be supervised
Sees work as a privilege	Sees work as a drag/
Has integrity	Corrupt/ lazy
Completes tasks alone	Leaves things incomplete
Has compassion	No or little compassion
Makes peace	Likes drama and fighting
Maintains truth	Untruths, half-truths & lies
Emotionally stable/healthy	Emotionally unhealthy
Open mind/mental alertness	Closed mind/mentally blunt
Positive/glass half full	Negative/ Glass half empty
Kind and loving	Unkind and unloving
Productive	Unproductive/
Works smart	Lazy or works hard/ overworked
Calm and in control	Angry / frustrated / irritable
Accepts responsibility	Blames others/ blame-shifting
Works to win / victorious	'Poor me' / victim mode
Has direction /inner GPS	Lost /without direction
Can lead others/ show the way	Mostly a follower
Trustworthy /dependable	Untrustworthy/ not dependable
Creative and innovative	Stereotype / boxed in
Can use technology effectively	Not technology literate
Understands communication	Not communication savvy
Spiritually open/ connected	Spiritually closed/disconnected
Open to change and progress	Resistant to change
Brings solutions to the table	Creates dramas and problems
Fun, exciting, and adventurous	Stagnated and dull
Disciplined and organised	Undisciplined and disorganised

Enjoyable to be around	Difficult to be around
Add in more aspects….	Add in more aspects …

Once you've gone through this list – you'll have a little more clarity of where you, your group, team, or company stand. You can change it by making new choices.

For more clarity subscribe to your Daily Power Tools for Power People.[15] A daily reminder of how to distinguish between real-me self and shadow ego-self will be delivered to your inbox.

Once you have read till here - you also qualify for a free Coaching session: Email us, and details of how to book your coaching session, will be sent to you.

Self-coaching is all about raising your awareness and gaining clarity. You take yourself to a new vantage point.

Here you can see much clearer.

Gaining more clarity

- How did you do on this list?
- How do you think your family/your spouse, partner, children did?
- How did your colleagues do?
- How did your team do?
- How did your company do?
- What can you change? Why? How?

Your To-do list

Now that you have read this far: Ask yourself the following questions:

Now that I have this new information:

- Who do I say I am? I am …
- Who do I say my shadow ego-self is?
- What do They look like?
- Where does my shadow ego-self come from?
- What influence does the shadow ego-self have in my life?
- Who do I say my real-me, authentic, soul-self is?
- What does it look like?
- Where does it come from?
- What influence does the shadow ego-self have in my life?
- What are the next steps I need to take?
- How do I get reconnected to my DNA Success-blueprint?

Make a list of things that need to be done

....
....
....
....
....
....
....
....

The next question you need to ask is; What do you want to achieve?

The title of this book is: Learning to coach yourself to ultimate success.

What is ultimate success?

Success means different things to different people.[16] More so, success has a totally different meaning to the authentic self than to the shadow ego-self.

- **Success and the shadow ego-self**

To the shadow ego-self success means having power positions and blingy possessions. The ego says, 'Look at me.' It struggles to maintain a social image of "I am Ok.'

It is constantly worried about what other people will say or if they have enough money or if they are good enough. They create a life that comes from a scarcity mentally.

It is a life of 'I want...' It is a life of hoarding for 'just in case'. Lots of 'stuff' is a symbol of success. Here a person feels that the Universe is closed, does not answer, and/or is absent. They feel lost, fearless, angry, and frustrated. Struggle and survival are paramount,

- **Success and the authentic self**

The authentic self needs places, opportunities, and experiences where it can express itself freely and apologetically

Because the authentic self is connected, it knows that it will receive whatever it needs from the Universe with effortless ease. There is a constant flow of everything good to you -in you- from you.

Here we find a different approach to success that includes manifestation. It includes having access to whatever you need when you need it. There is no worry, no concern, no fear, and anxiety. Whenever you need something, you ask for it and it shows up.

Here, success comes from an abundance of mind and an open heart.

- **Everyday living**

During the COVID-19 lockdown period, my kettle gave in. Working on a tight budget, like everyone else during the lockdown, I realised that at that moment, there weren't any spare funds available in the budget.

So, I put my request out to the Universe and said: I really need a kettle - now. Later I made an update and included. 'I really want a **red** kettle'.

In less than five minutes I got an SMS message from the local store where some of my books were being sold. Someone had purchased two books and the money was deposited into my account.

Immediately I went to a large retail store and lo and behold, there was a special on kettles in the appliance section.

The red kettle was on the front shelf.

Just think how it would be if our whole life functioned this way.

OoooOooo

WHAT NEXT?

This is only the beginning of this journey. It's only the tip of the iceberg. There is still a long way to go...

A series of *Authentic Living and Learning* books, courses, webinars, and coaching programs are available... and still growing

Follow series 1: Authentic living and leading

- Book 1: The authentic self. Who am I?
- Book 2. Coaching your self to ultimate success
- Book 3: Authentic Leadership: Recovering your DNA leadership-blueprint
- Book 4. Authentic Living. Success, Miracles and Spiritual Laws
- Book 5. Humanity's leap to authenticity. Where do you stand?

More books and courses in this series will be released later in 2021.
For books see: Amazon's Brenda Hattingh Page

Join our mailing list available here and get book one free

Get your free *Daily Power Tools for power People* delivered to your inbox here.

For courses see the Power Intelligence Leadership Academy here

Enrol for a five-week self-coaching course

oooOooo

ENROLL FOR A PERSONAL 5-WEEK COURSE.

Title: LEARNING TO COACH YOURSELF TO ULTIMATE SUCCESS

This will be one of the best investments you have ever made.

Background

Times have changed and we need to think on our feet. You can only be super successful and flourish if you know how to coach yourself and manage your inner dialogue. Very few people, especially leaders, know how to do this.

At the moment, we are also experiencing a genetic migration. Humanity is going through a transformation, right down to a DNA level. This means we also need to learn how to activate our DNA success-blueprint. The information on how to do this is now available.

Contact us if you would first like to book a free session

What will you learn?

In this beginner course of *Learning to Coach Yourself*, that runs over five weeks, you will learn:

- Who your real-me is and what your personal purpose is
- How to tap into and activate your DNA success-blueprint
- How to master your inner dynamics and create affluence
- How to create the next level of success and happiness
- How to overcome inner blockages and pitfalls
- To understand the psychology of money and affluence
- To understand the science and psychology of real success
- How to become an authentic leader and influencer
- How to create health, wealth and happiness that benefits everyone
- And much more…

What will you receive:

- E-book 1. Coaching yourself to ultimate success. Who

coaches who?
- E-book 2: Authentic living and leading. What is it and how to develop it
- Your personal workbook for your notes
- Five one-on-one personal coaching sessions via Skype, Zoom, or WhatsApp with Dr Brenda Hattingh.
- Three DNA-healing sessions
- A plan of action/map for the next season of your life.

Books available on www.amazon.com/books

Who should invest in this course?

Everyone who wants to move forward and create their best life. This includes people like you and me, leaders, teachers, parents, business-persons, couples …

How to book your *Course. Learning to coach yourself?*

Send an email to: info@powerintelligence.net. We will send all the necessary information to your inbox.

See our website: http://www.brendahattingh.com

BOOK DR BRENDA HATTINGH AS SPEAKER

To book Dr Brenda Hattingh as an exciting, entertaining, and inspirational speaker for your next event, or conference and training session, contact us by sending an email to:

Email: info@powerintelligence.net

See website: http://www.brendahattingh.com

oooOooo

BOOK DR BRENDA FOR LEADERSHIP TRAINING

Email us: info@powerintelligence.net

oooOooo

THE POWER INTELLIGENCE LEADERSHIP ACADEMY

See the courses currently available at the Power Intelligence Leadership academy

Website: https://power-intelligence-leadership-academy.teachable.com

WHO IS THE AUTHOR - DR BRENDA HATTINGH?

Dr. Brenda Hattingh is an international inspirational speaker, leadership coach and mentor and business, corporate and leadership consultant. Brenda invests her time in using personal and organisational power and success potential encoded as our unique DNA blueprint. This is a global first in personal and organisational training and development.

Brenda is committed to the development of a new level of consciousness with an awareness of the value of authentic living and leading. She focuses on assisting people, teams, companies and organisations – who are willing to bring their *best self* to the table.

As an author, Brenda brings to the table cutting edge information, books and training courses that include topics *like Power Intelligence – the intelligence of the future*, *New Success DNA*, and *New Leadership DNA*. She is Director of the *Power Intelligence Academy* and *The Academy for Authentic Leaders*. Brenda is also the *CEO of the Centre for Power Intelligence*

As an innovator, Brenda is committed to the development of a new generation of successful, innovative, inspired, thinkers and leaders. She speaks at events and conferences, presents workshops nationally and internationally, lectures at various universities and has published various books.

Her work is featured on TEDx Talks as Brenda introduces the next season of personal development and leadership training that includes tapping into your DNA-blueprint. Brenda is also the recipient of various awards including the *Professional Businesswoman of the Year Award*.

MORE BOOKS IN THIS SERIES

Available from. Amazon.com/books

CURING CORRUPTION

Corruption is one of the worst pandemics of our time. Corruption is in essence a mental-health issue and should be treated as such. Unfortunately, current strategies are failing because they don't address the fundamental root cause of corruption.

In the two books below, you will find all the necessary information for you to take in your place as part of the solution of the corruption pandemic.

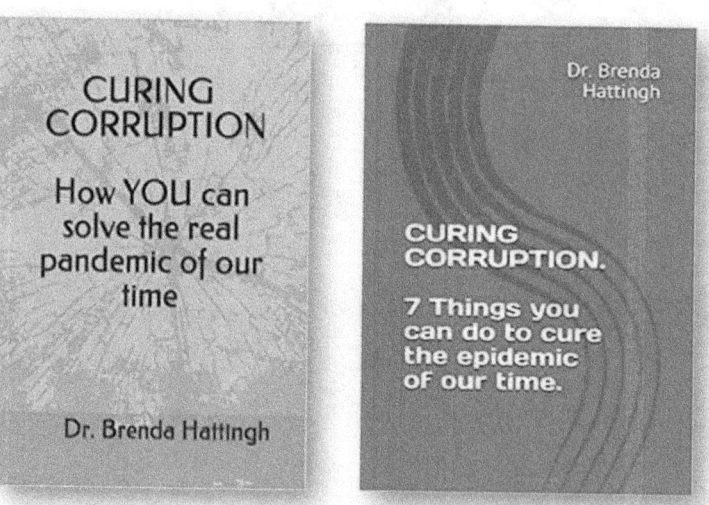

Books available: www.amazon.com/books

oooOooo

AUTHENTIC LEADERS IN ACTION

The world is in chaos and in dire need of real, authentic leaders. There are people who are awaking and are not afraid to stand up, take in their place, bring peace, build bridges, create a new vision of the future, and shine in their own unique way. These are our authentic leaders.

Such a man was Nelson Mandela.

We accelerate our own awakening, growth, and development by learning from those who went before us.

A course, *Ten lessons from Nelson Mandela...*, is available from https://power-intelligence-leadership-academy.teachable.com. Below you find two books with life-lessons from this iconic leader

. Available from. Amazon.com/books

REFERENCES

1. Holy Bible: St James version: I Corinthians 4:20
2. Holy Bible: Luke 17: 21
3. Hattingh, Brenda. (2014). *Seven steps to securing the Madiba Magic in life and leadership.* Currency Communications: Johannesburg.
4. Photo: Robert Cornelius Photography: www.robertcorneliusphotography.com
5. See website for more E-books and upcoming courses: Website: http://www.brendahattingh.com
6. See website: https://www.genome.gov/human-genome-project/What Still today new findings are emerging and evolving from this project
7. Hamers, Dean. (2005). *The God-gene. How faith is hardwired into our genes.* Amcor Publishers. New York.
8. For more on this scientific research see: Hattingh, Brenda. (2012, a). *New Success DNA. What you should know and how to develop it.* Currency Communications Int.: Johannesburg. Chapter 6.
9. See Holy Bible: Eph.1:5. The two spiritual families are represented by: Light or darkness—Christ or anti-Christ
10. Photos from http://www.cognitivebehaviouralcoachingworks.com
11. Hattingh, Brenda. (2012.). *New Leadership DNA. Developing enlightened leaders.* Currency Communications Pty.Ltd.: Johannesburg.
12. Hattingh, Brenda. (2012.a). *New Success DNA. What you should know and how to activate it.* Currency Communications. Pty. Ltd.: Johannesburg.
13. See the website for more information: http://www.brendahattingh.com Or make sure you are on our mailing http://eepurl.com/gO_d2P
14. See: *New Success DNA.* Chapter 10.
15. Link for you Daly Power Tools for power People http://eepurl.com/gIQl3H
16. Hattingh, Brenda. (2012). *New Success DNA. What is it and how to develop it?* Currency Communications. Johannesburg.

www.ingramcontent.com/pod-product-compliance
Lightning Source LLC
Chambersburg PA
CBHW070831220526
45466CB00002B/796